The Gam

When

Nigel Planer is an original ~~~~ ~~ the Comedy Store and Comic Strip. After studying African and Asian Studies at Sussex University, he went on to train as an actor at LAMDA, and has worked successfully in theatre, film, TV and audio since 1980.

His first play *On the Ceiling* transferred from Birmingham Rep to the West End. His second *Death of Long Pig* was premiered at the Finborough Theatre in London. He has had two plays – *On the Ceiling* and *The Magnificent Andrea* – broadcast on Radio 4.

His spoof theatrical biography *I, An Actor* by Nicholas Craig (with Christopher Douglas) is currently in its third edition. He has written novels *The Right Man* and *Faking It*, a best-seller about parenthood, *Good Enough Dad*, as well as publishing a short collection of poetry, *Unlike the Buddha*.

He regularly teaches and runs workshops for actors and for writers. In 2011 he was awarded an Honorary Doctor of Arts from Edinburgh Napier University.

The Game of Love and Chai
or
When Rani met Raj

By **Nigel Planer**

from The Game of Love and Chance by
Pierre de Marivaux

Methuen

First published in paperback by Methuen 2018

1 3 5 7 9 10 8 6 4 2

Methuen
Orchard House
Railway Street
Slingsby, York, YO62 4AN

Methuen Publishing Limited Reg. No. 3543167

www.methuen.co.uk

Copyright © 2018 Nigel Planer

Moral rights have been asserted in accordance with the Copyright,
Designs and Patents Act 1988

A CIP catalogue record for this title is available from the British Library

ISBN: 978-0-413-77815-4

Typeset by SX Composing DTP, Rayleigh, Essex
Printed and bound in Great Britain by Clays

This book is sold subject to the condition that it shall not, by way of trade or
otherwise be lent, resold, hired out or otherwise circulated in any form of binding
or cover other than that in which it is published and without a similar condition,
including this condition, being imposed on the subsequent purchaser.

Performance Rights Enquiries

All rights in this play are strictly reserved. A performance can be staged only
once a licence has been issued. All applications for performance must be
submitted to United Agents, 12–26 Lexington Street, London, W1F 0LE
[www.unitedagents.co.uk / info@unitedagents.co.uk]
before rehearsals commence.

Please note: the published text - which went to print before rehearsals
concluded – may differ slightly from that of the perfomances.

The Game of Love and Chai

Produced by Tara Arts

First performed at Tara Theatre, London, on February 28th 2018 (running until March 24th) and subsequently performed at The Lowry, Manchester from 29th to 31st March 2018, Queen's Theatre, Hornchurch from 18th to 21st April 2018, Belgrade Theatre, Coventry from 24th to 28th April 2018 and the West Yorkshire Playhouse, Leeds from 1st to 5th May 2018.

Original Cast

Kamala-ji   Goldy Notay
Sunny   Deven Modha
Rani   Sharon Singh
Raj   Adam Samuel-Bal
Sita   Kiren Jogi
Nitin   Ronny Jhutti

Directed by Jatinder Verma

Design by Claudia Mayer

LX Design by Andy Grange

Production Manager: Shaz McGee

Company Manager: Miranda Paraskeva

Deputy Stage Manager: Zoe Elsmore

Costume Supervisor: Hilary Lewis

For Tara Arts

Artistic Director: Jatinder Verma
Executive Director: Laurie Miller-Zutshi
Associate Director (Design):   Claudia Mayer
Associate Producer: Jonathan Kennedy
General Manager: Alexandra Wyatt
Marketing Manager: Jyoti Upadhyay
Digital & Communications: Katie Robson
Finance Manager: Sharon Zhang
IT: Hitesh Chauhan
Publicity Design: Feast Creative
Press: Mobius

Introduction

Nigel Planer's version of Pierre de Marivaux's classic farce brings to the fore the fascinating connections between East and West, connections that have enriched the theatrical cultures of both since at least the first embassy to the court of the Mughals during Elizabeth I's reign.

Shakespeare, ever in touch with the zeitgeist, incorporates the fabulous East as a dispute between Oberon and Titania over 'the lovely boy, stolen from an Indian king' in *A Midsummer Night's Dream*. John Dryden goes on to centre an entire verse-drama on one of these potentates – *Aurang-zebe*. Arguably, it was with the introduction of proscenium-arch theatre to Calcutta in the late eighteenth century – by, amongst others, David Garrick's brother – that Shakespeare, Richard Brinsley Sheridan, Molière and Marivaux, first stepped into the heat and dust of India. To Indian eyes, this revolutionary form of theatrical architecture opened the floodgates to a love affair that continued through Rabindranath Tagore, innumerable 'Parsee' theatre companies presenting adaptations of great European drama around India, Sybil Thorndike performing the title role in the Sanskrit classic *Sakuntala* at Drury Lane in 1912, Geoffrey Kendall's touring troupe of Shakespeare wallahs, and Peter Brook's version of *The Mahabharata* – 'the great story of mankind' – that took European theatre by storm in the 1980s. And, joyously, that revolution led to today's glittering Bollywood cinema, whose pioneers were all theatrical legends.

Nigel Planer's *Game of Love and Chai* brilliantly completes this circle of connections, employing Bollywood song and dance to delicious effect in Marivaux's clash of passion and class.

Jatinder Verma

The Game of Love and Chai

Characters

Kamala-ji	*A Widow*
Sunny	*Kamala-ji's son*
Rani	*Kamala-ji's daughter*
Raj	*Rani's suitor*
Sita	*Rani's cousin*
Nitin	*Raj's driver*

The scene is set in a well-to-do suburb in England, nowadays.

Act One

Mrs Kamala Arora's *house, in a well-to-do suburb in England, nowadays.*

Enter **Rani** *with* **Sita**

Rani For the last time, what bloody business is it of yours?? How dare you think you can speak on my behalf!

Sita Oh, sorry for thinking, even. Your Ma asks me if I think you'd like to get married, so I said yes! What's so terrible about that? I just thought for once, you might be like, a normal human being?

Rani Normal? A woman's not complete unless she's married, is that what you mean, uh?

Sita Well, yes actually, I do! I do, I do, I do! Why can't you just be like everybody else? Why have you always got to be better than everyone?

Rani Oh shut up Sita. You have such a big chip, you know?

Sita I'm fine being who I am. Confident. Strong. Uneducated, small, simple, but amazingly attractive . . . woman. [*Singing*] Double U, O, M, A, N! I'll say it again.

Rani You're just trying to wind me up now.

Sita Come on, babe, what's so wrong with marriage, eh? You know you want it really.

Rani No, I don't!

Sita You wouldn't say no.

Rani I *am* saying no. I'm very happy being a singleton. It's much more dignified.

Sita Oh yeah? Frustrated old Auntie more like. You'll end up a permanent kuwari.

Rani A what?

Sita Spinster! Old maid, fuss-budget, stick-in-the-mud . . .

Rani Alright, alright! God! You Indians! Besides, I don't want Ma getting the wrong idea and before you know it, the bottles of Ganges water will be out and she'll be buying plane tickets and we'll have half the bloody diaspora in our living room.

Sita Come on! This isn't some Shadi ki Filum! Your Ma-ji is very modern woman.

Rani I don't want to be the one to let her down in a year's time.

Sita So you will let her down today, and refuse to even meet the guy, is that it? You're not making sense, babe.

Rani Oh I don't know, Seets. Men are always such a disappointment, you know?

Sita Well . . . I heard that this wallah – your fiancé . . .

Rani Sita!

Sita . . . this guy, whatever, is very successful businessman. Intelligent, got all these qualifications, MA, PhD, MSC . . . RSI. MRSA. Sounds perfect. Appropriate match for you, no?

Rani Appropriate? Yuch! What a terrible word. And please don't use the 'auspicious' word either, or I'll scream.

Sita You're lucky to find a guy who wants to do things properly these days. Most girls would have him [*She snaps her fingers.*] . . . just like that. And that! And that! I'd have him.

Rani Enough!

Sita Even if he didn't want me, I'd have him. Chained to the bed, I'd have him. Intelligent, successful, what else was it? Oh yes, good sense of hu-ooge bank balance. All the qualities in one male package. One male package, Rani, think of that. Packaging. A real hottie.

Rani God, you are so mercenary, Sita. Poor guy, I say.

Sita He's got to be high status for you. Only Alpha-Male will do for my coz.

Rani Sita! It's not like I have some kind of Man-Index you know?

Sita You do. And apparently . . . he is really good-looking too.

Rani Yeah, well good-looking is actually a drawback.

Sita What! What! What are you talking about, doll?

Rani Good-looking men are always the most vain.

Sita Oh! He can be as vain as he likes if he's got something to be vain about. Sunny said he's fit, this fellow. Built like a tank, Sunny said. So hot you could fry an egg on his fender.

Rani You are so shallow, Sita. Good looks and a six pack are not going to make a marriage last.

Sita But you could spend a few years finding that out, isn't it? [*She laughs*]

Rani What about kindness? What about honesty, eh? Honesty. Remember that? And that's before we even get onto alcohol abuse, aggressive tendencies and sport!

Sita OK, so some guys can be a bit Aspergers-y. So what? They just need a bit of sensitive handling, if you know what I mean. Huh! Bit of hand work. Huh!

Rani And sport!? What is it about sport? I mean, football! What's that about?

Sita Er . . . ripped guys? Pumping and sweating and getting sexed up and . . .

Rani No, I mean football *culture*. League tables and fanatical team loyalty. They're like little boys. And cars? Eh? Top Gear??

Sita Oh, is that about cars? I thought it was about Matt le Blanc.

Rani I am so bored listening to their endless drone about engines, competitions, equipment, teams, speed, scores . . .

Sita OK, so, you don't like the usual manly stuff, but what about smoothy uncle Prakash then? He's not into any of that, is he?

Rani That's because smoothy uncle Prakash is a misogynistic, weasly, two-timing slime ball. That's why.

Sita Don't hold back Rani. Why don't you say what you really think of him, doll.

Rani Prakash! Aaargh! What a great husband he turned out to be! I went there the other day and he comes over to me with his arms wide open – 'Aie! Beti! Baithie, baithie' – like he's the nicest guy in the world. But his poor wife, Nandini's upstairs, red eyes, tissue box out . . . again. And we all know why; dirty bastard's been touching up his interns again. That's the kind of state I could end up in. I felt sorry for her, Sita; imagine *you* feeling sorry for *me*. Yuch, disgusting! I couldn't bear it. Too humiliating. You see, that's what it means to be married.

Sita What? Sorry, I didn't hear any of that. I stopped listening after the word husband.

Enter **Kamala-ji**

Kamala-ji Well! Good morning, Rani my love! Sita has told you, huh? He's coming over today. Today, only! I just got a letter from his father this morning. [*She holds up the letter.*] I don't know what's wrong with old-fashioned email these days, but... Exciting, huh? No? What's the matter? Something wrong my darling?

Sita Just men, Auntie-ji. They're two-faced, cheating, emotionally stunted and boring. Every single thing that's wrong in the world is down to men. War, famine, pollution, corruption, it's all men and she wants nothing to do with them and that's what's the matter.

Kamala-ji What? What's all this gibberish? Has she been reading *The Guardian* again? Rani? Explain.

Rani I was just telling Sita that all the wives I know are either miserable, frightened or bored. That's all. No big deal.

Sita Yes, she was telling me how uncle Prakash-ji, despite providing a Honda Civic for each one of his children, is sometimes a bit on the slimy side.

Kamala-ji Well, Uncle Prakash is not such a good example, Sita, if you knew the whole story, but . . . [*To* **Rani**] So you're nervous, huh? Understandable. All the more so, as you don't even know this Raj fellow. Very successful in pharmaceuticals, huh?

Rani What's that got to do with it?

Kamala-ji Yes, yes, you're quite right. Sorry. Nothing at all. Nothing at all.

Sita And he's extremely good-looking, which is a drawback. According to Rani.

Kamala-ji A drawback? How's that? Huh?

Sita I'm just repeating what she said. She's read all the feminist books. She's the one with 'a education'. I wouldn't know anything about anything. Sorry I spoke even.

Kamala-ji Oh, Rani dear. Look sweetie, I know you too well to think I could make you do anything against your will. Huh? This isn't some big 'arranged' thing, huh? We don't have to do everything by the rules any more.

Rani But what about Papa-ji?

Kamala-ji Papa-ji would've just wanted you to be happy. This Raj's father was your Papa's oldest friend, but I absolutely forbid you to do anything just because you think your Papa would've wanted it. He's gone, Rani dear and we're still here. We carry on. That's all there is to it. If this Raj isn't to your liking in any way, you just have to have a quiet word with me, huh? Chupuke chupuke. And he'll be sent packing.

Sita Just like in *Pardes*, eh, Auntie-ji? [*Sings*] Chupuke chupuke. Do dil, mil rahe hai. Magar. Chupuke chupuke. [*Two hearts are meeting, but, softly softly. (from the film 'Pardes')*] Oh, Shah Rukh!

Kamala-ji Shut up Sita. Stop it.

Rani Yes, shut up, Sita.

Kamala-ji Actually I prefer Ranvir now.

Sita [*launching into the louder bit of the song*] Saanson mai badi begaraari, Ankhon mai kai rat jage.

Kamala-ji Sita! [**Sita** *stops singing*] [*To* **Rani**] I've never seen this Raj either – for all I know he may be an idiot. But from what I've heard, I think he is definitely worth considering. In the end, you know . . . you just have to be yourself.

Rani Oh Ma, you're so good. And since it's *you* telling me to be myself – in the end – I will be.

Kamala-ji [*laughing*] You better be. In fact, I order you to be.

Rani And I obey, ji. I will be myself. But, would it be alright to be a little hmm . . . something else . . . in the beginning?

Kamala-ji Well it's pointless me trying to stop you doing whatever you want my dear. Always was.

Sita Yeah, soft parenting can lead to alcoholism, you know?

Kamala-ji Thank you Sita. Always so helpful. [*To* **Rani**] So . . . explain yourself. What little scheme do you have in mind?

Rani When Raj gets here today, I want to check him out a bit without him knowing! Put him through a test or two.

Kamala-ji Hmm. This sounds like something I shouldn't really be told about.

Rani If Sita pretended to be me, just for a short while, I could get a good look at the guy. And I'll be her.

Kamala-ji Well, it's a tricky game, the game of love. You might be taking on more than you bargained for, but why not, my darling. Sita, can you be Rani for a day?

Sita Easy-peasy, look. [*She puts on an exaggerated face and attitude like* **Rani**, *superior and despondent.*] And how about this? [*She walks about a bit like* **Rani**.] See? What do you think?

Kamala-ji [*looking from one to the other in mock surprise*] Goodness me! Shabash! I can hardly tell the difference myself!

Sita [*impersonating* **Rani** *perfectly now*] 'Seets? Would you do my nails for meeting Raj? You're so-oo good at it.'

Rani I don't do that! Do I?

Sita [*still as* **Rani**] 'And Seee-eeets, could you get your things off the floor in my room? And can you take all your hair out of the plughole, you're blocking it up . . .'

Rani Alright Sita, no need to rub it in.

Kamala-ji Well come on then you two, if you're going to do it, time to get dressed up. It takes you both so long, he'll've come and gone by the time you're ready.

Rani I don't need to dress up to be Sita. Anything from Primark will do.

Sita Oi! Zara, thank you very much! But, I'm going to wear . . . your gold choli.

Rani Oh, Sita, that was grandma's.

Sita [*grandly*] Now now. You must call me Rani from now on. With respect, yuh? It's appropriate that I should be meeting my man in grandma's best gold choli. It did the trick for grandma, na? [*Getting very grand now*]

Rani [*to* **Kamala-ji**] Ma?

Kamala-ji Well if you're going to play a game you might as well play it properly. Let her wear the gold choli. Coh! You kids are so old-fashioned nowadays.

Sita That's what I said. [*To* **Rani**] Come on, Sita. And mind your manners.

Rani Alright Rani, madam-ji. Whatever you say. I'll get you back for this later.

Sita Chalo! [*Exit* **Sita**

Enter **Sunny**

Sunny Hey sis! Looking forward to meeting the hunk, eh? I hear he's got property in San Francisco, Delhi, Dubai and Derby! Quite a catch, eh?

Rani Oh catch up, Sunny. Ma, tell him. I have more important things to do. [*As* **Sita**] Right doll, time to get sprauntzed up, innit? [**Kamala-ji** *laughs.* **Sunny** *is puzzled.*]

[*Exit* **Rani**

Kamala-ji Leave her alone, Sunny. She's got things to do.

Sunny [*in a colonial voice*] What's going on, Mater, old girl? Anything I should know about?

Kamala-ji I'll tell you. But you have to keep it to yourself.

Sunny Yeah, 'course.

Kamala-ji Promise?

Sunny I promise, I promise. Sounds good. Is it about this bloke who's coming round today to see Rani?

Kamala-ji Yes it is. But . . . he's going to see her . . . in disguise.

Sunny Oh, coo-ool! What like fancy dress? Are we all going to dress up? Can I be Beyoncé?

Kamala-ji No. Don't be stupid. Look, can I trust you? Look at this. [*Checks they are not being overlooked*] Look at what this boy's father wrote in the letter. [*She reads from the letter.*] 'My dearest Mrs Arora-ji, warmest etc . . . bla bla bla etc etc,' . . . ah here . . . 'just to warn you, my son's got it into his head that he'd like to have a discrete look at your daughter first, before showing his hand, as it were, and so he might be turning up at your place pretending to be the driver or some such.'

Sunny   Ha! Oh man, that is so cool! Rani's going to hate that! It's brilliant!

Kamala-ji   Listen, listen to the rest of it . . . 'Personally I think it's a damn fool idea, but I suppose it does at least show that the boy is taking this thing seriously. After all, we did agree that they have to actually like each other . . .'

Sunny   I love it when things go cra-a-azy!

Kamala-ji   There's more, there's more. 'I'm certain your lovely daughter will pass his stupid-boy test with flying colours. Oh and his driver will be pretending to be him, just so you know . . . All my best regards, etc . . .' Well? What do you think? Shall we tell Rani? [*There is a moment's pause while they both consider, then dismiss, this.*]

Both   Naaaa.

Sunny   It'll be such fun seeing her making a complete moorkh of herself.

Kamala-ji   Well no, Sunny, it's going to be a bit more interesting than that. Because your oh-so-clever sister has devised an identical plan herself, with Sita, so that they can 'check out' this fellow and see if he cuts the mustard. What do you think of that, huh?

Sunny   Oh lush! Oh Man! This is going to be chaos! Let me get my Go-Pro. I don't want to miss a single frame. Stick it up, this'll go viral.

Kamala-ji   Yes, why not. We're going to have them wandering about all day, play-acting being in love. It's priceless!

Enter **Rani**
wearing flashy clothes that don't fit/suit her

Rani   This is ridiculous! Sita has nothing, nothing in her wardrobe that isn't chavvy. I look like something off TOWIE!

Sunny   Very sexy, sis! [*Sings*] Irresistible! So modern! Wow! You should go to work like that.

Rani   Sunny, I'm a solicitor.

Sunny That's what I meant. Do some soliciting.

Rani So Ma has told you everything?

Sunny Oh yes! Everything! The whole lot! It's great! One thing? His driver will definitely fancy you dressed like that!

Rani [*impressed*] Oh, he has his own personal driver, does he?

Kamala-ji I don't know. Yes, maybe. He is a very busy, successful man. Pharmaceuticals.

Rani Well, if the driver does fancy me, that's good too. He's bound to have all the dirt on his boss – what he's really like – and I can tease the information out of him.

Sunny Tease is right, sis, dressed like that! You better be careful that the boss doesn't fall for you as well.

Rani That would prove my point, exactly. Men. So predictable. So tacky.

Sunny Oh yes, guys like that always like to take advantage. Excitement of the forbidden. The lure of power. Steamy ego trips for fat cats . . .

Kamala-ji Alright, Sunny. Enough, huh? [*To* **Rani**] And I think any man in his right mind would find you attractive whatever you were wearing, my dear. [*A buzzer goes. She goes to the entryphone.*] Ooh! Ssshh, ssshh. Yes? [*An indistinct voice on the other end*] Yes, do come in. [*She pushes the entry button.*] [*To* **Rani**, *excitedly*] The driver's here already! Where is Sita?

Rani Still getting ready. Hair, make-up, jewellery, the lot. She's taking this all a little too seriously. She's turned my room upside down. Oh God! Ma?

Kamala-ji Steady now. It'll be fine.

Sunny Hey Rani? [*in Aamir Khan accent*] All is vell. [*from the film 'Three Idiots'*]

Enter **Raj** *dressed casually*

Raj Mrs Arora-ji?

The Game of Love and Chai   Act One   11

Kamala-ji Yes, that's me.

Raj It is an honour to meet you Madam. [**Raj** *touches* **Kamala-ji***'s feet.* **Kamala-ji** *jumps back a little surprised. The others look impressed.*] Madam, I hope you received our email. My boss . . . Sahib, sends his apologies, he's been delayed at work. But he sent me on ahead to pay his respects for him. He hates being late. Ever.

Kamala-ji You are too kind. Well, Sita, what do you think of that, huh? A bit of old fashioned formality. Bhariya, bhariya. Good, good.

Rani [*finding it funny, but really taken with him from the moment she sees him*] Yes, a bit of foot touching – always does the trick with the oldies. Well done.

Raj [*looking into* **Rani***'s eyes, intensely*] Tradition has so much to offer, don't you think? [*He bows his head respectfully to* **Rani**, *and brings his palms together.*]

Sunny Hold on, hold on, hold on! This is not Rani. This is just our poor cousin Sita, from India? She's staying with us?

Rani [*charmed*] No don't stop. I'm OK with a bit of tradition every now and then.

Raj [*he's transfixed by* **Rani** *as much as she is by him*] I think some respect is due, whoever you are.

Kamala-ji [*can't repress her laughter any more*] Ha! Ha! Ha!!

Sunny Well now we've got all that gubbins out of the way, what's your name?

Raj Bhubaneshwarasanapatharam. Sir.

[*They are all nonplussed.*]

Sunny Bhubanesha – what?

Rani Bhubaneshwar like the town?

Raj . . . sanapatharam.

Rani . . . sanapatharam.

Raj Bhubaneshwarasanapatharam.

Rani Bhubaneshwarasanapatharam. So be it!

Raj But you can call me South.

Sunny What? Oh I see, South. You don't look dark enough to be South.

Raj Too pale for my name. I know. People always say that.

Rani Well, South, you can call me Sita. Or Seet.

Raj Or sweet?

Rani Oooh. Cheeky. Sweet. I quite like Sweet.

Raj Or sweety? [**Rani** *laughs at his daring.*]

Sunny Wait a minute. Before you two get carried away. Sita? [*Stalling*] Erm . . . remember, you said you would be my girlfriend? Remember? You promised me?

Kamala-ji Sunny, cool it.

Rani You can call me whatever you like, South.

Raj [*to* **Sunny**] I'm sure she can make up her own mind about what she wants me to call her.

Sunny Now look here, what makes you think you can come in here, and talk like that to my . . . to my girlfriend . . . what happened to traditional?

Kamala-ji Sunny, keep a lid on it. Chup.

Raj Only joking. She laughed when I said it, so I thought it was alright.

Rani Yes Sunny! What are you talking about?

Sunny Fine. I didn't realize he was being 'ironic'. How clever. What a comedian.

Rani Sunny. Boyfriend. Don't be so possessive. Just because I laugh at someone else's witty remarks, doesn't mean I don't think *you're* funny. You're a complete joke in fact.

Kamala-ji The main thing is that Raj is on his way. We must go and tell 'my daughter'. As for you . . . 'Sita', show this young man where the bedroom is? [*Reaction*] The bedrooms!

Kamala-ji [*cont.*] I mean the bedrooms. Where our guests will be sleeping. See you later, Mr Bhubaneshwa . . . South.

Exit **Kamala-ji** and **Sunny**

Raj [*aside, furious with himself*] Fuck!! Fuck fuck fuck! I knew this would happen! Idiot! Why can't I keep my big mouth shut. Sweety! Sweety?? What a dick! Why does she have to be so attractive? Same old story, I end up fancying the wrong one – some down-market, no-hope cousin – and make a complete twat of myself in front of her. Dad'll kill me.

Rani [*aside*] God my brother is a pillock sometimes. I don't know what he thought he was doing. Girlfriend! This driver seems to fancy himself rather a lot. Confidence is a very attractive quality actually. And useful. Easier to trick him into spilling the beans on his boss.

Raj So, tell me Sita, what's your cousin, the brilliant Rani, like? I hear she has a very successful career in the Law.

Rani Oh yes, mostly corporate and property. Important stuff, you know? She's quite an independent woman actually. Doesn't really need a husband, you know?

Raj She must be very confident in her looks also, going around with a cousin like you.

Rani South? You are so cocky!

Raj Yes, I am. Sorry.

Rani You think that flattery will get you somewhere?

Raj No it's just, I've got to report back to my boss what I see.

Rani And?

Raj This Rani must be a real scorcher because what I see is a very attractive cousin.

Rani South!! Enough with the Eve-teasing!

Raj Sorry I didn't mean to step over the . . .? [*Trying to be working class*] It's just, it's just where I come from, everyone says it like it is, you know? We call a spade a spade. We were

Raj [cont.] simple, straightforward people. Hard. And so poor. I was just lucky my boss picked me out of that hell-hole and . . .

Rani Oh yeah. Same for me. 'course. I owe my whole life to my cousin Rani and Auntie Kamala-ji.

Raj We didn't have much in the way of education, money . . . toilets, you know . . .

Rani Oh mate! I *so* know what you're talking about. Like, 'toilet ek prem kahani'? Right?

Raj What?

Rani Toilet, a love story. Isn't that the latest film or something?

Raj Oh yeah. I knew that. So there was always a lot of banter, you know? Like, piss-taking banter? That's all. It don't mean nuffing.

Rani No, of course not. What?! I'm cool with that. 'course! So, just mates.

Raj What?! Yeah 'course, what else did you think?

Rani [*aside, fanning her face*] Wow! What a guy! Outrageous! [*Out loud*] So tell me, erm . . . has your boss done his star chart? Do you think he and my cousin will be compatible?

Raj Does anyone bother with that these days?

Rani Yeah right. No. Exactly.

Raj My boss is not interested in Astrology. He wants to make a love marriage.

Rani Aah, how lovely.

Raj You know how these rich, posh guys are these days. They think they can do away with all that family stuff and just do what their heart tells them. It's bad.

Rani Oh. Yeah right. It's bad. My stupid cousin Rani wants the same. Love marriage definitely. Stupid. Tch . . .

The Game of Love and Chai   Act One   15

Raj   But I've had my star chart done.

Rani   So have I. 'course.

Raj   'course.

Rani   What's yours like?

Raj   I'll show you mine if you show me yours. We might find *we're* well matched! [*They laugh a little too much at this.*]

Rani   What do you mean we?

Raj   Yes, we might find *we* were meant for each other.

Rani   Ha, ha, ha! If we could understand the bloody things that is!

Raj   Exactly! I haven't a clue. It's all rubbish anyway. Let's not look at them.

Rani   No, let's not. [*They're both relieved, but can't stop staring at each other.*]

Raj   So a love marriage it is then. For us.

Rani   Will you stop it?! Stop it with your banter! Tell me more about your boss. Is he an honest man?

Raj   Honesty's his middle name.

Rani   Would he treat my cousin with respect?

Raj   Respect? That's his other middle name.

Rani   Oh. Strange parents. But what would it be like waking up with him beside you every morning for the rest of your life?

Raj [*looking in **Rani**'s eyes*] He'd look in your eyes – and say . . . God you're beautiful.

Rani   South! You're insatiable! Will you stop that right now! If you go on like this I shall have to leave. [*She moves as if to go.*]

Raj   No, no, Sita! Wait! Stay!

Rani [*aside*] Masterful. Hmm.

Raj I did have something to say about my boss . . . [*She turns back and looks him straight in the eyes.*] . . . but I've forgotten what it is now . . .

Rani [*dreamily*] Yes, I'm beginning to lose the thread of the conversation . . .

Raj [*trying to collect himself*] We were talking about astrology and, and love marriages, and middle names and waking up in the morning beside you. That was it.

Rani South! It's getting quite rude, now, you know. Goodbye. [*She turns to go again.*]

Raj No, no, it is about my boss. Honestly.

Rani It better be.

Raj It's just, I can't think and look at you at the same time. Sorry.

Rani Careful, South.

Raj [*looking at the floor*] OK, my boss, my boss, is . . . a good guy.

Rani Well, he can't be all bad if he rescued you from that terrible hell-hole you were in.

Raj Oh yeah. That. Exactly.

Rani So he's a good judge of character.

Raj Oh. Thank you so much for saying that. That is *so* kind of you. You seem like a very kind person, Sita. [*He says her name as if it is magic. They are looking in each other's eyes again.*]

Rani Well, yes I am. South. [*She says his name as if it were amazingly romantic.*] To listen to you for so long, for a start. [*PAUSE*] I don't know why I can't seem to drag myself away.

Raj No. Nor me.

Rani No. I'm still here. Looking at you. It's ridiculous. Goodbye. South.

Raj   Goodbye. [*Neither of them have moved.*]

Rani   I'll just have to find out for myself what your boss is like.

Raj   When you meet him.

Rani   Yeah, maybe.

[*Suddenly, a Bollywood-style mobile ring-tone chimes out, making them both jump.*]

Enter **Nitin**

Nitin   [*dressed in over-the-top clothes, carrying a case, car keys and a flash mobile phone which he switches off*] Ah! Here you are South, old chap! Southy! Southy boy! How have they been treating you?

Raj   They've been treating me, Sahib. [*Under his breath to* **Nitin**] *What* are you wearing?

Nitin   Good good good! Did they show you where to park the Porsche? Capital, capital. Here's keys. [*Tosses* **Raj** *some keys.*]

Raj   . . . Porsche? What Porsche?

Nitin   Fetch my case.

Raj   You have your case.

Nitin   No, this is my *other* case. My Mitthai case! Sweeties!! [**Nitin** *whips open the case to reveal it is stuffed with Indian sweets.*] I always think sugar and dairy products are best way of saying – this marriage is ON!!

Raj   Oh dear.

Nitin   These are for my mother and my WIFE!

Rani   Are you sure you don't mean Mrs Arora-ji and her daughter?

Nitin   Arora, daughter, mother, wife, same thing! I've come to get married, they want me to get married; it is settled. Only missing thing is signing of a piece of paper. But what's that in this modern day and age?

Rani The most important decision of your life?

Nitin Yes but – 'when once one has wended one's way in the world, one will always be wedded by one's word, wouldn't one wager'? Wah! Wah! Wah!

Rani [*in a low voice to* **Raj**] He's certainly got a way with words.

Raj Got away with murder more like.

Nitin What's that, my lovelies?

Rani Nothing. Just saying I'll go and tell Mrs Arora-ji you're here.

Nitin Why don't you call her mother like I do? Because that's what she is, isn't it?

Rani Not yet she isn't.

Raj She's right, Sahib-ji, the marriage hasn't happened yet.

Nitin But I'm here to make sure it does.

Raj Just hold off the big talk until the actual marriage. Sahib. Sir. With respect.

Nitin Ah, what is time? Today, tomorrow, eternity, what's the difference?

Rani Single, married, divorced, you're right. No difference at all. I'll go and tell 'mother' that you have invaded, sorry, arrived.

Nitin And my wife, don't forget. Tell my wife also. And what's your name, pretty little thing?

Rani Sita. I'm Rani's poor cousin.

Nitin Charming, charming. And what do you do around here? Hmm? Run the house the way the mistress likes it? I bet you do!

Rani As you say.

Nitin Oh, we're going to get on like house on fire, I can tell. So, tell me; how do you feel about *me* being family? Hmm?

Rani I find you . . . most amusing.

Nitin Well played, well played. [*He pretends to be a cricketer batting.*] You've not seen anything yet. This is going to be first rate! First rate!

Rani And so modest.

Nitin Modesty, my best cover-drive.

Rani But if you'll forgive me, I must leave you now. I'll get Mrs Arora-ji; I'm sure she'll appreciate your jokes more than I can. I'll fetch her.

Nitin Bring it on, sister!

Rani [*aside*] Whatever this guy's got, I hope it's not catching!

[*Exit* **Rani**

Nitin Alright!! Not bad, eh? Cousin really likes me, don't you think?

Raj You complete and utter dickhead!!

Nitin What? I thought I did really well there.

Raj You promised me you'd do this properly! That was ludicrous! I gave you clear instructions! I couldn't have made it any clearer.

Nitin You gave me fifty quid and said wear something upmarket.

Raj I meant a sensible suit and tie, not something out of Saturday Night Fever. God, what an idiot I was to rely on you.

Nitin Listen Sahib, I'll have you know I run a very respectable business-ji. Kabhi Kabhi is a very reputable mini-cab transportation option.

Raj Oh, save me.

Nitin [*launches into the jingle tune for his Cab company*] Jab kab chahiey! Kabhi Kabhi Chahiey! Kab kabhi chahiey?? Hamesha, hamesha hamesha hamesha!! [*When you want a cab, you need Kabhi Kabhi, when do you want Kabhi? Every time, every time! etc*]

Raj No, no, no no! What monster have I unleashed?

Nitin Did you like the suitcase bit? Brilliant touch that! All my own work. What do you think it's going to be? A five lakh wedding? Gifts separate of course.

Raj I don't believe this.

Nitin Price tags still on the presents.

Raj Will you take this seriously!? Jerk.

Nitin Alright I'll try harder in the next scene; I'll be all serious. In fact, I could be depressed, d'you think that'd work? 'Oh God, this is torture! Marriage! Commitment! It's all so depressing!'

Raj Uh, do what you like. I'm completely out of my depth anyway. What are we doing here, Nitin?

Nitin If all else fails, cousin's quite a looker. [**Raj** *fumes*] Raj? Mr Sharma Sahib? Sir? Best customer? What is it?

Raj Shut up will you? Here comes Mrs Arora.

Enter **Kamala-ji**

Kamala-ji A thousand apologies for keeping you waiting, but they only just now told me you were here.

Nitin Madam-ji, a thousand is far too many apologies! I give you nine hundred and ninety nine apologies back. For you to use as you see fit.

Kamala-ji I hope I won't be needing them.

Nitin Aha ha! Depends how well behaved you are, don't it! Naughty lady! As for myself, I am at your service, Ma-ji. [*He quickly corrects himself.*] Not that I am a servant. No, not at all. No, I am a top master, like what you are. Mistress, I mean.

Kamala-ji Right. Well, we've been awaiting your arrival with great anticipation.

Nitin I would have come earlier with South, but you know how one gets so ponky after work and gym! I felt I just had to go and freshen up in my twin-headed Jacuzzi shower, you know how it is.

Kamala-ji Ponky?

Nitin Rank, cheesy, stinky. But have no fear, smell that! [*He shoves his armpit in* **Kamala-ji**'s *face.*] Nice, eh?

Kamala-ji [*recoiling*] What is that?

Nitin Febreze! I doused myself in it before coming out. For the younger ladies, you understand.

Kamala-ji [*almost choking on the smell*] Well . . . I'm sure they'll be . . . entranced. I'm afraid my daughter is still getting dressed. She won't be long. Would you like a little refreshment until she comes down, huh? . . . Chai?

Nitin . . . Oh! I never refuse a drink. 'Mine's a Mohito'. No seriously, just a Chai Latte Toddy with cinnamon top. Regular. Oh South? Go and make yourself useful in the servant's quarters, why don't you. Polish shoes or something.

Kamala-ji Oh no. We don't have live-in staff here. Why not let him stay?

Nitin Stay? Well, he might get a bit tetchy and bored with the high-brow conversation what we will be having. Have you got some videos he could watch? Something simple? About cars? He likes them. It's all he knows about. [*To* **Raj**] Brrum brrum. [**Raj** *groans, disapprovingly.*]

Kamala-ji I'm sure he'll be able to find something to occupy himself.

Nitin Oh, alright, let him stay. [*To* **Raj** *again*] Little Barfi.

Kamala-ji And here she is!

Enter **Sita**

Suddenly, **Sita** *appears in full Sari with jewels and bells on her ankles. She has tilak on her forehead. She is carrying a recording device; ghetto blaster on her shoulder, or perhaps just her iPhone. She stands for a second or two, looking as alluring as she can.*

Nitin, *who had his back to her, is spun round by the sight of her. He is instantly frozen to the spot.*

Nitin   Aaah! What vision is this! [**Sita** *bats her eyelashes seductively*.] Is this a Durga that I see before me?

Sita   No babe! This is the real thing. In the flesh. Get ready to be blasted.

Sita *puts the recording device down and switches it on, with deliberation. There is the sound of fake wind and a cow bell or two. Exactly like from the beginning of the song 'Tujhe Dekha, To yeh jana Sanam,'* [*from the film 'Dilwale Dulhania Le Jayenge'*]. *Entranced,* **Nitin** *sings the opening line of the song* [*but in a higher key, the key of the actual song which is about to be played*]. *Their eyes are locked as they walk towards each other, as if in a big field of corn.*

Sita   [*singing*] Tujhe dekha, to yeh, jana – sanammm.

Nitin   [*singing*] Pyaara hota hai, divana – sanammm.

Sita   [*singing*] Ab yaha se kaha jaye hammm. Teri baahon mai mar, jaye – hammm.

Nitin   Oh man! She even knows the lyrics!!

Suddenly there is music. It is the opening swirling violins from 'Sola Button Meri Choli Hai' [*from the film 'Darr'*].

Enter **Sunny**, *dragging a reluctant* **Rani** *with him*

He approaches **Sita** *from behind . . . and helps by wafting her sari a bit, as if the wind is blowing her.*

Kamala-ji   Well I think she looks lovely.

Sunny   This is my sister Rani!! Phwoooaar, as they say.

Rani and **Raj**   Whatt?? Oh please! I don't believe this ... [etc]

The singing on the track starts up and **Sita** *mimes to it: 'Meri Ma ne Sola Button Meri Choli Hai.'* [*'My mum sewed sixteen buttons on my blouse.'*] *It's a pretty old-school Bollywood routine.* **Sita** *dances and mimes as seductively as she can for* **Nitin***'s benefit. She is very committed to the whole performance, perhaps too committed. Every now and then she has to tuck her sari back in, she is not used to wearing one. As the number picks up,* **Sunny** *joins in with her. He has also made an effort and is quite good at mugging and miming to the lyrics. When the chorus arrives,* **Nitin** *can't help himself and joins in too.*

Rani   Oh God, this song is about forty years old. So retro. Pathetic.

Raj   I can't believe I'm seeing this.

Nitin [*as he whisks past them*] The film came out in 1993 actually.

Kamala-ji   One of my favourites. [**Kamala-ji** *joins in the dance with* **Sita** *and* **Sunny** *and* **Nitin**.]

Everyone is having fun except **Rani** *and* **Raj**, *who are embarrassed. The others dance around them and force them to join in the dance too which they do, reluctantly and badly.*   [*Exit* **Rani** & **Raj**

Sita *sings and dances an exit from the song, followed keenly by* **Nitin**. *Then* **Kamala-ji** *peels away and exits too, leaving just* **Sunny** *dancing with no sound track.* **Sunny** *realizes he is alone and leaves*

[*Exit* **All**

Lights indicate time pass

Enter **Kamala-ji** *and* **Sita**

Kamala-ji   Well? What is it Sita, dear?

Sita   I have to talk to you for a minute Auntie-ji.

Kamala-ji   Yes?

Sita   I've got to tell you exactly what's going on, just so you know. Then you won't be angry with me.

Kamala-ji   Angry? Why would I be angry?

Sita   Before I tell you; you did agree to Rani's disguise idea, didn't you?

Kamala-ji   Yes . . . .

Sita   Right. So we all thought it would just be a bit of fun, didn't we? But it isn't, it just got serious.

Kamala-ji   Serious? How serious?

Sita   Well. I know it's wrong to praise yourself, but, well actually, I can be quite sexy, you know.

Kamala-ji   I'm sure you can, Sita, and what's so wrong about that?

Sita   I think Rani should tell him who she really is before things get out of hand. I think we should stop the game now, because if we leave it much longer, he won't want Rani at all.

Kamala-ji   Goodness, so you don't think my daughter has enough allure?

Sita   It's my allure I'm worried about. It's out of control, it's gone ballistic, it's luring all over the place. It's pouring out of me and luring things I didn't mean to lure. And you've got to stop it.

Kamala-ji   Oh good grief! Sita, I never knew you had so much allure! [*She laughs*]

Sita   You think I'm joking. This whole thing is going horribly wrong.

Kamala-ji   Don't worry about it, Sita. Keep calm and carry on, huh?

Sita   I am telling you Auntie-ji, it's all happening so fast. This Raj guy doesn't hang about. He's already said he loves me, and that was just over the chai and ladoos. By supper time he could adore me. You can say whatever you like, I won't be able to stop myself, by tonight he might . . . worship me. There is a point of no return you know.

Kamala-ji And what is so wrong with a bit of worshipping? If he likes you that much then perhaps he should marry you, not Rani.

Sita What? What? What, what, what? You mean you'd be OK with that?

Kamala-ji Only if it's what you want, my dear. Do you like him too? Does he stir up your passion?

Sita Oh, ho, ho, be careful, Mrs Arora, Auntie-ji. If my passion gets involved in this, the guy won't know what hit him. He'll be quivering jelly on the floor, begging me.

Kamala-ji Begging, I like the sound of that. I definitely think you should say yes, if he begs you.

Sita And you wouldn't mind me getting all that fortune? And the Porsche? And the house in Derby? We could have little dogs. And holidays in Scotland.

Kamala-ji No, not at all, Sita dear. You just do what you have to do. Now tell me about Rani. What does *she* think of this Raj fellow, huh?

Sita I've hardly had the chance to talk to her because the guy's been all over me since he got here, but from what I can see, I don't think she is very happy about it. She's gone all quiet. I think any minute now, she's going to ask me to turn him down for her.

Kamala-ji Oh no, don't do that, huh? Promise me? I think she should spend a little longer observing him, just to make sure. And what about the driver? Is he behaving himself?

Sita He is a strange one. He's following Rani around like a sad little puppy.

Kamala-ji Oh, she must hate that. Doesn't she tell him to get lost?

Sita Well no . . . she blushes.

Kamala-ji Really! Surely not? Our Rani? She's more than used to being followed around by good-looking young men.

Sita Auntie-ji, she blushes. I saw it.

Kamala-ji She must be furious with him then, huh?

Sita Whatever.

Kamala-ji Well, next time you get to talk to her, tell her you think this driver's just working on her, to try and influence her decision about his boss. And see if that makes her angry.

Sita I don't want her snapping at me.

Kamala-ji If she snaps at you, we'll know she really likes him. Oh look, here comes Raj . . . looking for you, apparently.

Enter **Nitin**

Nitin Ah! There you are my little saptapadi! My seven steps of fire! The foot on my foot! I've been asking everybody where you were. I am just yearning to get married. Dear mother-in-law. Mother. Mummy. I am totally at your disposal. Totally. Dispose of me.

Kamala-ji Good, well, thank you for that. I'm sure I don't want to dispose of you. I will leave you two alone. You'll have a lot to talk about before making your decisions.

Nitin Have no fear, I can talk and decide at the same time.

Kamala-ji I'm sure you can, but all the same – slowly. Take it slowly.　　　　　　　　　　　　[*Exit* **Kamala-ji**

Nitin Slowly, slowly! It's easy for her to say that, she's old! We're young and bursting with sap, aren't we my bucket of love? How can we wait? Let us tie our clothes together now! [*He tries to tie their clothes together. She swats him away.*]

Sita Tsk. You can't be that much in love with me, we've only just met. You're just showing off because you want to impress me. Go on admit it.

Nitin No way, baby! It's a slam dunk! The moment I clapped my eyes on you, my love was born, that exact moment it popped out!

Sita Oooh!

Nitin Then when you first looked at me it was a little baby, crawling around looking for a cuddle.

Sita Aaah.

Nitin And the first sound of your voice made it stand up . . .

Sita Oh!

Nitin . . . on its own two feet. And start shouting; 'I want my mummy! I want my mummy!'

Sita Oh, poor thing. There must be something I can do for it.

Nitin There is! It's such a lonely little love for a girl who won't even hold its hand.

Sita Here you are then, here's my hand, but only to keep you quiet you understand.

Nitin [*kissing her hand fervently*] Ah, what relief from your dear, dear handy! Oh! Your digits! Eight of them! Ten, counting thumbs. [*He puts her fingers in his mouth one by one.*] Dear lovely handy-hand! Ah! It tastes like delicious dip! Oh, if only we had more prawns!

Sita OK. Stop there for a moment?

Nitin But I'm so starved of your dip.

Sita Alright, but let's keep it within the bounds of sanity shall we?

Nitin Sanity! Sanctity! Can't you see I've lost it all, staring into your delicious eyes.

Sita Yup. My eyes are up here, actually.

Nitin Yes, them too.

Sita OK, you can go on now. It's hard to believe that it's just me that's the cause of all this craziness.

Nitin [*trying to kiss her*] All you have to do is look in the mirror to believe it.

Sita Actually, I think we'd look a bit silly like this in the mirror.

Nitin Ah! So modest. So down to earth! So . . . earthy! Earthy, moist, deep!

Sita Oh look, here's your driver.

Enter **Raj**

Raj Could I have a word with you, Sahib?

Nitin No. [*To* **Sita**] Damn staff! Always interfering!

Raj Sahib? Ji?

Sita [*to* **Nitin**] Well go on, see what he wants.

Raj I have one word to say, only.

Nitin Alright. But if you say two, the third one will be 'You're Fired!' Yes! And er . . . that's the fourth word, obviously.

Raj [*in a low voice to* **Nitin**] Come here, twat!

Nitin [*in a low voice to* **Raj**] That's not a word, that's an insult . . . [**Raj** *hits* **Nitin**] Ow! And a smack . . . [*To* **Sita**] Dear future wife, forgive me, it's business. And in business you have to learn to take the knocks. It's all part of the game, you know . . .

Sita I understand. You'd better go and do some more negotiating then.

Nitin Thank you my love. [**Raj** *drags* **Nitin** *away from* **Sita**.]

Raj [*in a low voice*] What the bloody hell do you think you're doing? You're supposed to be mooning about, dreamy and sad, not rutting like a frenzied dog.

Nitin [*loudly*] Yes, my friend, quite so.

Raj [*still in low voice*] You've got to get me out of here, fast. This Rani girl's not right for me, the whole thing's a fiasco. [*He starts to leave.*]

Nitin [*loudly*] Ha ha ha. But don't you worry about it, my good man. And you may leave now. [*pushing* **Raj** *away*] Now. Leave.

[*Exit* **Raj,** *resentfully*

Nitin   Ah! My dear shadi-shudi-pie! So sorry. Now where were we before we were so rudely interrupted by that ghastly uncouth type? I've forgotten what I was going to say. Now my mind is cluttered chock-full of mundane, everyday, businessy things. Oh yes! My love for you, which is not mundane and everyday at all. But it *is* the business! *You* are the business! My business! So when are you going to join me in this love corporation?

Sita   I do want to but . . . but my hands are tied.

Nitin   I can go with that. Whichever way you like it.

Sita   No. Oh, how can I explain?

Nitin   No need. I'm open-minded when it comes to you.

Sita   I'm not exactly what you see. You see?

Nitin   Always keep that bit of mystery. I LOVE it! I'm intoxicated by it! I'm on fire! Masta Masta!

Sita   No, I mean there's a lot less to me than meets the eye.

Nitin   You mean you're padded? Oh my dear, dear lady, I would love you whatever chuddies you wear.

Sita   I just wish I was in a position to reveal my feelings?

Nitin   You look fantastic whatever position you're in.

Sita   If only I could find the right words . . .

Nitin   Perhaps I can help you. The right words are 'I . . . love . . . you . . .' Repeat after me; 'I . . . love . . . you.' Easy.

Sita   God, you're insatiable! Well here goes. [*She mumbles it quickly.*] I love you.

Nitin   Sorry couldn't hear that.

Sita [*a little louder*] I love you.

Nitin Louder!

Sita [*shouting*] I LOVE YOU!

[*They both look around, to see if anyone is coming*]

Nitin Oh I'm so happy! Let's go to Shimla! No! Let's go to Switzerland and roll around in the snow, and then let's run around the London Eye with a wind machine! Dance India Dance! Season Three!

Sita Yes, but what about later? When you get to see the real me. When you see who I really am, [*almost crying*] I'm afraid your love might wither and die.

Nitin Actually when that happens, believe me, it's you who will be disappointed.

Sita I'm not as great as you think I am, you know. When you get to know me.

Nitin What about when you get to know *me*? The real me? The normal me? He's complete rubbish.

Sita But that's not your fault is it?

Nitin Exactly! We can't help how we were born.

Sita I would have chosen you, whoever you were.

Nitin Oh! Same! Same! I was just going to say exactly same!

Sita It doesn't matter who we are does it? Really?

Nitin Of course not! Even if you weren't a qualified solicitor and daughter of a reasonably rich mother-in-law, I'd still feel like this.

Sita Oh that's so beautiful!

Nitin Even if you worked in Waitrose as a checkout girl. No, Lidl! Even if you worked in Lidl as a checkout girl, I'd still think you were the cutest thing.

Sita I so hope you mean that.

Nitin Let's not just hope, let's swear! Let's swear to love each other for ever and ever, even though we don't know who we really are! Then we've covered all bases really, haven't we.

Sita Oh God! I can't believe this is happening. This means much more to me than it does to you. I swear it! I swear it!

Nitin [*kneeling down*] I swear it too, I swear it too.

Sita I can't believe that it's me that's driven you to this. I feel so guilty. Stop it, stop it, get up please. I can't bear it.

Nitin *leaps to his feet and tries to seduce* **Sita** *with a song. He mimes to 'Tu Cheez Badi Hai Mast Mast'* [*from the film 'Mohra'*]. *It's a very sexy number full of hip movements.* **Sita** *joins in. They get carried away with it.*

Enter, after a little while, **Rani**, *looking at them cynically*

After a little bit more dancing, **Nitin** *and* **Sita** *stop, embarrassed when they realize* **Rani** *is watching them. She has ruined their fun.*

Sita Oh hello little cousin Sita. Did you need anything?

Rani I need to talk to you, Rani.

Nitin Yeah. Look, darlin'. Fifteen minutes? We're kind of busy here, know what I mean?

Rani I need to talk to my cousin, Rani, ji. It's important.

Nitin OK, but we were like, given strict orders to get to know each other before getting married, right? And you're kind of, messing that up?

Sita Can't you come back later, Sita?

Rani No.

Nitin Ho! Feisty lady! I like that.

Rani [*aside*] Oh yuch! What a prize-winning, puffed-up, prat.

Nitin So what is it that you want to talk about?

Rani Oh, you know, girls' stuff.

Nitin Oh, girls' stuff. What, lip-gloss, selfies, kittens, that kind of thing?

Rani Yeah, that's right. And men, of course. We talk about men.

Nitin Aha! Right! I know what you MEAN. OK, I'll take a little walk and leave you two girls to it. But don't be too long will you . . . [*To* **Sita**] My biddy, buddy, budu. My splashy-splishy puddle. Of love I mean.

Sita We won't.

Nitin Au revoir, sayonara, toodle-pip, milenge . . .

Sita Soons . . .

Rani [*sarcastically*] Laters.

[*Exit* **Nitin**

Sita [*heaving a big sigh*] Aaah.

Rani [*misunderstanding* **Sita**'s *sigh*] Yeah, right. What a creep, yuh?

Sita I didn't think he was that bad.

Rani Well, you wouldn't would you? Each to her level, I suppose. He's nowhere near good enough for me.

Sita You haven't given him a chance.

Rani Are you out of your mind? One glance at him is enough to know he's a complete cretin. But evidently Ma doesn't agree, because she's skulking around avoiding me, hoping I'll come round. Look, you've got to get me out of this. I want you to turn him down and send him away.

Sita Sorry Rani, but I can't do that.

Rani Can't? What's stopping you?

Sita Your Mata-ji, Mrs Arora forbade me to turn him down. Just now.

Rani Forbade you? What nonsense! My Ma never forbade anything in her life, everyone knows that.

Sita Well, she forbade me.

Rani I'm putting you in charge of telling this pharmaceutical oaf what I really think of him. Put it however you like, I don't want to see him again, he's an idiot and there's an end to it.

Sita Well, he seems really nice to me. Like *really* nice . . .

Rani Well, I'm telling you he's a moron.

Sita All your Ma-ji asked was that you take some time to get to know him. He's gorgeous when you get to know him, honestly.

Rani I hate him already. I don't need more time to hate him some more.

Sita Ooh. Hate him eh? That's a strong word. A very passionate word.

Rani Oh please!

Sita What about his driver? Mmm? What about him? Aren't you just repeating what he's told you to say? That driver's been working you, hasn't he?

Rani How dare you say that! The driver? South?! What's it got to do with him? It's got nothing to do with him! Ha! What makes you think that? That's ridiculous!

Sita I think he's just a smooth-talking lady's man. I think he's playing you like a gigolo.

Rani Give me a break, Sita. I've hardly spoken to the man. But I have to say from the little I do know, he seems a very sound and sensible guy.

Sita I think you've just fallen for his smarmy-charmy looks. It's funny, I thought you were smarter than that.

Rani Oh I see! Now it all comes out! It's really good we changed places isn't it, because now I can see what you really think of me! Trying to get me to defend a perfectly decent man – who's perfectly capable of defending himself by the way – just so you can say I'm typical gullible female.

Sita Oh sorry. I didn't realize it mattered so much to you. Since you seem to care so much about it, I won't say another word. My lips are sealed.

Rani What are you insinuating, cousin?

Sita I've never seen you in such a state, and I'm just a bit puzzled, that's all. But, I'm sure you must be right, Rani. You're always right.

Rani Oh my God! That's outrageous! What's got into you? That is so . . . so . . . oh . . . I can't . . . [*She sobs a little.*]

Sita Rani lost for words. There's a first. Truth always hurts the most. What really matters is that everyone else thinks what you think. So alright, he's a really decent guy. There.

Rani That is so unfair! I don't care what anyone else thinks of the stupid driver, alright? I don't care what I think of him! Which I don't! I don't think of him, alright! I don't think about anything any more. What's happening?

Sita You've changed.

Rani *I've* changed? I've *changed*? Oh go away, leave me alone.

Sita I was leaving only.   [*Exit* **Sita**

Rani God I'm still shaking. Bloody Sita! How dare she! Why would I defend a guy like South? Some smart-ass lothario who thinks he's God's gift. I wouldn't. Would I . . .?

Enter **Raj**

He stands to one side, trying to pluck up the courage to speak to **Rani**.

Rani [*looking at* **Raj**] . . . No. Oh God there he is! Oh, look at him! Sita's wrong about him. He couldn't be playing with me. Could he? Now, Rani, watch what you say, don't take your temper out on him, when he probably doesn't deserve it. Innocent until proved guilty. Oh it's you, hi. How ya doin', bhai?

Raj Sita, I don't know whether you've been trying to avoid me, but there's a bone I need to pick with you.

Rani Yeah, tight. Spit it out, mate, namsayin'?

Raj Are you alright?

Rani What d'you mean?

Raj Well, you're talking rather strangely.

Rani It's just the way I was brought up you know, namsayin'? Sort of Urban, like.

Raj Sure, if you say so. Look Sita, let's not waste what little time we've got left by talking crap with each other.

Rani What do you mean? Are you leaving? So soon? With your boss? I mean is your boss leaving? With you? And you're driving him?

Raj Yes. I'm afraid so. Would you have a problem with that?

Rani Me? Naaooo. No big deal to me. What do I care?

Raj And it's no big deal for me too? Is that what you think?

Rani What made you think I would be thinking about you? I wasn't thinking about you.

Raj Well I can't get you out of my mind.

Rani Now look here . . . South, isn't it? I'll only say this once; you can stay, you can go away, you can stay and go away and come back again for all I care – any of those things, staying, going, coming back, I won't mind either way. OK? And I'm not saying this because I hate you. Nor do I particularly even like you. I mean that would be mad, to feel anything either way for you, wouldn't it? I'm only saying this to be completely straight with you.

Raj [*destroyed*] Oh. I thought . . . ? I don't know what to say . . . I . . . I don't know what to do with the rest of my life now.

Rani What stupid talk is that! [*Aside*] Oh! Now he's made me feel sorry for him. The poor man. What have I done? [*To* **Raj**] Now come on, get a grip, South. I'll 'friend' you on FB, OK?

Raj No. That's ridiculous. I can't bear this. I hate goodbyes at the best of times, but this is impossible.

Rani [*playing for time*] You said you had a bone to pick with me. What was that?

Raj Oh, nothing important. I just wanted to see you.

Rani Out with it.

Raj It was just, I thought you'd been bad-mouthing me to Rani. Saying I was trying to spoil her chances with Raj.

Rani Who told you that? Rani? I never said any such thing.

Raj Right well, that's alright then. See, it was nothing. I suppose I'd better go then.

Rani If you have nothing else to say, we have no more reason to be together.

Raj I feel such an idiot. Let me look at you for one last time. [*He sighs.*]

Rani Do you know, you'll look back on this one day and laugh. So will I. [*She tries and fails to laugh.*]

Raj And now, you're mocking me. Fair enough I suppose. I don't even know what I'm doing any more. Bye.

Rani You're doing the right thing. Bye. [*She can't bear to see him go.*] So, your boss, he's leaving too then? You'll be driving him, will you? [*He comes back.*] In a car?

Raj Yes, that's right. In a car.

Rani So, erm . . . what sort of a car do you drive?

Raj Oh, the motor? It's erm . . . a flash one . . . erm . . . a GT, erm . . . Turbo X nine mil. Erm . . . CBT.

Rani Wow! A GT Turbo X nine mil!

Raj CBT.

Rani Yeah, CBT. Wow! I love those cars.

Raj I keep telling him about his carbon footprint, but he won't listen.

Rani Yeah. No. How interesting.

Raj [*gathers himself*] Look I have to leave or I'll go insane.

Rani Oh! Don't go insane! Don't go insane!

Raj I should have left the very first moment I saw you.

Rani [*aside, fanning herself*] I must forget everything he says. I must forget everything he says.

Raj If you only knew the tricky situation I'm in, Sita.

Rani It's not half as tricky as mine, I can assure you.

Raj And you don't even particularly like me, you said. Right?

Rani Heaven forbid!

Raj And you don't even hate me. Not even a little bit.

Rani Absolutely.

Raj So you have absolutely no feelings for me whatsoever?

Rani None. Nope. Nothing. Not a thing. Up here, down below. Not my type.

Raj Tell me again. Put me out of my misery.

Rani Oh! This is impossible. Do you *have* to put me through this?

Raj I'm struggling Sita, I'm struggling to believe you. Help me, Sita. Tell me again. Tell me you feel nothing. When I am fighting this so hard. So hard. Please. [*He falls to his knees.*] I'm on my knees, Sita.

Enter **Kamala-ji** *and* **Sunny** *during the following lines, standing a bit away watching*

Rani Oh no. That's all I need. Get up now please. South? Someone will see us. This is all my fault. I'll say whatever you like. What do you want me to say? Alright, I don't *not* like you.

Raj I know I'm not much of a catch. Just a driver. But if I was, for instance, a relatively well-off businessman with lots of qualifications, would you feel anything then?

Rani No, it's not that. Look, it's not you, it's me. I'm sorry. Oh, what can I say to make it better?

Raj You could say that you can't live without me.

Rani Will you stand up if I say that?

Raj Only if it's true.

Rani OK then, yes. That's what I think.

Raj What?

Rani That. What you said. The can't . . . live . . . without . . . bit.

Kamala-ji [*approaching*] Well it's all going jolly well I'd say. Shame to interrupt. Bravo! Shabash!

Rani Oh! Ma . . . [*Correcting herself*] Auntie-ji. I can't stop this man from kneeling down. I didn't do anything, I swear. He's just gone out of control.

Kamala-ji I must say you look absolutely charming together. Now, Sita, I need a word with you in private. Would you mind, Mr South? I'm sure you can pick up where you left off, later on.

Raj [*getting up*] Ji.

Kamala-ji And South? What's this I hear about you smacking your boss, poor Raj-ji.

Raj Me, Madam-ji?

Kamala-ji Yes, you. Evidently, respect is not your most prominent quality.

Raj I don't know what you mean. I was just . . .

Kamala-ji Later, later.

[*Exit* **Raj**

Kamala-ji Not like you Rani my dear, huh? Looking at the floor. What happened to all that self-esteem?

Rani You're imagining things, Ma.

Sunny Something spooky is definitely going on though, definitely. Doo-wee-ooo [*He makes a science fiction noise.*]

Rani In your mind, Sunny, going on in your filthy little mind. All that's going on in mine is complete incomprehension of what you two are on about.

Kamala-ji Has this Mr South been putting you off Raj? Who, I must say, seems like a perfectly reasonable option to me.

Rani That driver man putting me off Raj?

Sunny Yes, the rather good-looking and keen driver, Mr South. The genuflector.

Rani Your good-looking and ever so keen driver, Mr South has not even mentioned his useless and ridiculous boss, Raj to me, in all the brief conversations I've had with him.

Sunny In all of the four hours that you've known him.

Kamala-ji Well that's not what we heard, Rani. We heard he's been saying bad things about Raj. Which may have clouded your matrimonial judgement. That sort of thing.

Sunny Yeah.

Rani The only thing that's turned me off Raj is Raj himself, OK? With his stupid case of sweets and his ludicrous shiny clothes. Has Sita been talking to you? It was Sita wasn't it? She's poisonous that girl.

Sunny Alright, alright, no need to get all hot and bothered.

Rani I am sick and tired of these stupid, chavvy clothes. Can I get changed now?

Kamala-ji Oh no, don't do that. Leave a bit longer, huh? I went along with your game didn't I? Now you go along with this a bit longer and please, suspend your judgement of this Raj fellow, until you get to see the bigger picture.

Rani Hello-o? You're not listening to me are you? I am an adult. I am perfectly capable of forming my own opinions based on the evidence.

Sunny So this guy, South has got nothing to do with your sudden romantic aversion to Raj?

Rani [*inflamed*] What is this? Why is everyone using all these strange expressions today? Romantic aversion? Matrimonial judgement? Somewhat indiscrete? We're not in some eighteenth century French comedy, are we? [*There is a moment's puzzled pause while they consider this possibility.*] You both seem to find it all very amusing, anyway.

Sunny Oh Rani. Why so hyper-sensitive today? I don't know what's got into you. Some magic voodoo juice. Can I have some?

Rani Excuse me! What about the crap that's got into you. You seem to be talking out of your arse, Sunny.

Kamala-ji [*sharply*] Enough, Rani, huh? Sita was right, you really don't seem yourself today. It's as if all your brain functions have gone . . . South.

Rani Sita! My toxic cousin?! This is so unfair. I just think that our game got a bit out of hand and the poor man, South, got caught in the crossfire, that's all. Which I didn't think was fair, so being a decent human being I decided to help him, OK? Because I don't like to see people getting hurt. And look at the thanks I get for that.

Sunny   I can't see any wrong in that. [**Sunny** *and* **Kamala-ji** *are giggling.*]

Rani   And it amuses you obviously, that there are some kind people left in the world. Stop making fun of me, you bullies.

Kamala-ji   Alright, calm down, Rani.

Rani   I am perfectly calm!

Sunny   [*in accent*] All is vell. All is vell. [*singing from the film 'Three Idiots'*]

Rani   I just want to calmly say that you are wrong. Sita's a cow. I've had enough. And I don't know why we're still talking about it. Now I really am upset.

Kamala-ji   Well whatever the truth of the matter is, I think young Mr South, may very soon find that he has been fired.

Rani   What? That's ridiculous! Toxic cousin Sita arranged that did she?

Kamala-ji   I wouldn't be too concerned if I were you. The chap has been practically harassing you since he arrived. I would've thought you'd be quite relieved to get rid of him, no?

Rani   No, no, it's all my fault. He just thinks I'm Rani's flirty little cousin and fair game. It's like I've been playing with the poor guy's feelings.

Sunny   I never realized you were such a convincing actress, Meryl. Really 'in' the role.

Rani   Shut up Sunny.

Kamala-ji   Yes, we saw him kneeling down in front of you just now. Kneeling! And then he made you say that, what was it? . . .

Sunny   That you didn't – not – like him.

Kamala-ji   That's it, you didn't – not – like him. [**Rani** *is speechless and chokes.*] Shocking, he made you say that before he would get up again. Who knows what he would have made you do if we hadn't turned up.

Sunny Definite low-grade harassment.

Rani Oh very clever, both of you! You two are enjoying this far too much. You're so transparent.

Kamala-ji The only thing I ask of you, Rani my precious, is that you wait a little longer before you turn down Raj. You'll thank me in the end, huh? Trust me.

Sunny I predict you'll end up marrying Raj, and living happily ever after. But only if he fires that awful driver, South.

Rani Alright! Enough! Now, leave me alone!

Kamala-ji It is up to Raj to decide what to do with his employees. Come on, let's go. Chalo, Sunny, chalo.

Sunny Bye Rani. No hard feelings.

[*Exit* **Sunny** *and* **Kamala-ji**

Rani Ah! I feel dreadful! What's happening to me? I don't know who to trust any more, least of all myself.

Enter **Raj**

Raj Ah! Sita! At last! There you are!

Rani Oh no, not again! Look, I can't do this anymore, OK?

Raj [*stopping her from going*] I need to talk to you one last time. It's about your Auntie Kamala and her daughter.

Rani Go and tell *them*, then. Every time I see you, I end up getting upset. Leave me alone.

Raj It's the same for me, when I see you, but listen, it'll all be different after I've told you what I have to say. Honestly.

Rani Oh, here we go. Well, OK, talk then. I am listening. Two minutes.

Raj Can you keep a secret?

Rani Me? I got A* in GCSE trustworthiness. And I went on to major in Confidentiality at uni. Get on with it.

Raj I am only telling you this because I respect you.

Rani Don't say that. Sounds like you want something from me.

Raj No, I want to give you something; . . . the truth. So, here goes; you know how much I feel for you.

Rani I knew it. Go on, tell me more about your feelings again. Take your time, South, you've got one minute and three seconds left.

Raj I am not South.

Rani Eh?

Raj I am not Bhubaneshwarasanapatharam.

Rani Oh. That's good. Who are you then?

Raj Ah! Sita! You've no idea how good it feels to get that off my chest! Aaaghh!

Rani OK, Mr Neanderthal, I'll try again. Who are you then?

Raj Is anyone coming?

Rani No.

Raj It's all gone so pear-shaped, I owe it to you to come clean.

Rani Yes, well done. Jolly good. Now . . .

Raj Ohhh! This is so hard. OK, here goes; the guy who's talking to your cousin Rani? He's not who she thinks he is either.

Rani [*impatiently*] Well come on, say it, who is he then?

Raj An unlicensed cab driver I have an account with.

Rani Right.

Raj And . . . and, I am Raj Sharma.

Rani Right OK. Yeah, I see. That makes sense.

Raj I just thought it would be a good idea to get a quiet look at Rani before, you know . . . there's so much pressure. My family, you have no idea. Any way it was a stupid thing to do. I can see that now. I think Rani is awful. Stuck up, over-dressed, pretentious. I can't stand her. I mean, no way! And what's worse is, she's fallen in love with my dickhead of a driver. What am I going to tell them all? And what can I say to Rani? 'Yeah look, I'm sorry but I'm in love with your down-to-earth cousin, not you.' And what about Mrs Arora-ji and my dad, and . . . . [**Rani** *stops his mouth with a full on kiss. It lasts a few seconds. Then she plucks herself away from him, leaving him breathless.*]

Rani [*aside to audience*] I don't think I'm going to tell him who I am.

[*Blackout*

Act Two

Lights up on the scene exactly as it was before.

[*It is one second later.* **Raj** *is still breathless and dizzy from the kiss.* **Rani** *is still facing the audience*]

Rani [*to the audience*] . . . because . . . I want him to want me for who I am, not because of some . . . arrangement. [*To* **Raj**] My apologies Mr Sharma-ji. I don't know what came over me.

Raj [*recovering still*] No, no Sita. No need to be so formal with me. No apologies needed, believe me.

Rani So, you were saying; you have a problem with your family and traditions and your dad, and how to explain yourself to my poor cousin and Auntie-ji.

Raj Oh Sita, it's a nightmare. I've really got myself into a messed up situation. What am I going to do?

Rani I'd hate to put you through any more stress. That would be cruel. And I am human, only.

Raj Oh what a relief! Thank you thank you thank you. I knew you'd be understanding. Another one of your amazing qualities.

Rani Oops, someone's coming. Listen, don't do anything for the moment, I'm sure I can think of something to help relieve your . . . situation.

Raj Oh, would you? You're an angel. [*Exit* **Raj**

Rani [*aside*] I wonder what I would've done if it hadn't been him.

Enter **Sunny**

Sunny Oh there you are, bahin. Having a little cry, were you? Look, I'm sorry we were so horrid just now. But [*like Baldrick*] I thought of a *cunning plan* that might help you.

Rani Never mind that! Listen to this!

Sunny What?

Rani South is not South, he's Raj.

Sunny Which, what? Which one do you mean?

Rani Him, South, Bhubaneshwarasana... Thing. He just told me. Just now!

Sunny Which one? The nutter or the schmoozer?

Rani Oh, Sunny. Catch up!

Sunny No. Explain it properly.

Rani I need your help, Sunny. Remember you told him I was your girlfriend?

Sunny Yeah, but I was only joking.

Rani Well, how do you think you'd feel if I really was your girlfriend?

Sunny [*grimaces*] Uhh. Pretty disgusted actually. I mean that would be incest apart from anything else.

Rani No, I mean, if I, *Sita*, was your girlfriend, and some other guy was breathing all over me like that?

Sunny Oh you mean like the driver?

Rani Like Raj! Raj! The driver is Raj.

Sunny Like Raj! Aah, I get it. Well, he'd be welcome actually.

Rani What?

Sunny Well, I don't really fancy you that much do I?

Rani Oh Sunny! Behave!

Sunny [*like Austin Powers*] Oh Sunny, be – hayve! No I get it, I get it. Make him a bit jealous, eh? Possessive. [**Rani** *nods*] Get him all steamed up and desperate eh? Why?

Rani I've got to make sure he's the right one. Just put him through one more test. Come on, let's go and tell Ma! All systems are go!

Sunny OK, whatever you say, Sis. Sounds bonkers, and also a bit gender discriminatory, but, hey, what's new.

[*Exit* **Sunny** *and* **Rani** *from one side*

Enter **Raj** *and* **Nitin** *from the other side*

Raj *is beating and kicking* **Nitin**, *and smacking him round the ears.*

Nitin Oi! Sahib, please! Health and Safety! Health and Safety!

Raj You stupid! Dumb! Idiot!

Nitin Ow! I'll take you to a tribunal! Abuse of authority! Position of trust! Ow! Ah! It's domestic violence!

Raj Are you taking the piss, you little shit! I'll give you a damn good thrashing! No, a thrashing's too good for you. They should bring back flogging!

Nitin I operate under a strict no bullying policy! Ow! And that's name calling! It's racist.

Raj Racist? How is it racist?

Nitin Tell you what – would you like me to go and fetch a suitable hard object, like a brick say?

Raj A brick would be just the thing – to smash over your stupid head.

Nitin [*taking out his mobile*] Would you mind repeating that, I didn't quite get it on here. For my lawyer, you know and the *Mail on Sunday*. Ow!

Raj You complete bastard!

Nitin Complete bastard is alright. Thanks for that one. A lot of husbands are complete bastards and I'm just about to get married aren't I.

Raj How dare you! You think I'm just going to stand by, while you fraudulently marry this honest woman's daughter? *In my name?*

Nitin Now that's a good idea. I like where you're coming from on that. It's a good starting point for negotiation. I think a deal's possible here. Just to remind you; the girl is crazy about me, she goes all trembly when I come near.

Raj The moment she knows who you really are, never mind trembling, she'll be shaking with anger.

Nitin Right. Right. We'll see about that. I'll go and tell her – right now! Then you'll see what kind of love you're dealing with! And Mr Sharma, Sahib? I hope we can still be friends when I'm married. You must come over for dinner some time. Nothing too formal, you know. Ow!

[*Exit* **Nitin**

Raj Uunnhhh! This has all gone spinning out of control. Oh Sita. [*He sighs*] When you're with me, it all seems to make sense. Where are you?

Enter **Sunny**

Sunny Hey, 'South', I want a word with you.

Raj Oh no. What next? How can I help, Sir?

Sunny Have you been coming on to Sita?

Raj I have been talking to her, if that's what you mean. I talked about me and her having a relationship, as a matter of fact.

Sunny I see, and how did she react to that?

Raj She laughed, mostly.

Sunny Would that be laughing at you for being an idiot, like 'huh, huh huh'? Or would it be more of a 'ha, ha, ha, haaa'? [*He tosses his hair back to imitate a woman flirting.*]

The Game of Love and Chai   Act Two   49

Raj Actually, it's more of a 'hehr, hehr, hehr, hehrrrr.' [*He imitates a very sexy come-on laugh with seductive eyes.*]

Sunny What? She gives you a 'hehr, hehr, hehr'? I find that hard to believe. Cocky fellow aren't you?

Raj Well, it's whatever you're 'endowed' with, isn't it? Sir.

Sunny Oh very hard. And no doubt she falls for your tough guy impression.

Raj I don't do impressions. Did you come here just to insult me, or have you got something to say? You have a problem with me talking with Sita?

Sunny Ooh, insecure already. Better check that, my friend. Could turn jealous. Could turn ugly. Could turn jelly jealous.

Raj You'd know all about jelly, wouldn't you.

Sunny [*acting tough*] Alright, here it is. You stay clear of her. Leave her alone. I don't want you seeing her. At all. Or I can't guarantee your safety. Got me?

[*They are eyeballing each other.*]

Raj Oh yeah. I've got you alright. I've got you right here. [*Indicates the palm of his hand.*] And I'm not going to let go.

Sunny [*gulping, a little scared*] I'm just saying, that's all.

Raj So you fancy yourself as a contender, do you?

Sunny Yes, I do. I fancy myself quite a lot. Actually.

Raj And how about, Sita? You think she fancies you back?

Sunny She might do.

Raj Have you asked her?

Sunny She hasn't actually said anything yet. But she'd be well up for it, if you know what I mean.

Raj Have you even told her how you feel about her?

Sunny Not in so many words. But I think she's got a pretty good idea of how hot I am for it. You know. So watch out! Because if you try it on with her, you'll have me to contend with, alright?

Raj Sure. Whatever you say.

Enter **Rani**

Sunny Oh, there you are Sita. Phew.

Rani What's wrong Sunny? You seem a bit, a bit, sweaty.

Sunny Nothing, nothing. I was just having a few words with South, here. Telling him what's what, you know.

Rani Were you two quarrelling?

Raj This bloke told me he fancies you, Sita.

Rani Yes. I can't help that, can I?

Raj And he told me not to come near you. He got quite aggressive.

Rani Oh dear. Well, we'd better stop meeting like this then, hadn't we?

Sunny I know I can't stop him from loving you, Sita, but I don't want him running round telling you he does. Is that so wrong?

Rani To be frank, he has become a bit repetitive, darling.

Sunny Not any more. I think it's time you moved on, South. Yi haa!

Raj No. I'm waiting for her to tell me to go.

Rani Well, you can stop waiting now. Time's up.

Raj Are you serious? You've got something going with this guy? I don't believe it.

Rani Oh so now you're going to tell me who I can and can't talk to, eh? Who my friends can be? Typical controlling man.

Raj What?

Rani Listen, buster, I can talk to whoever I want to talk to, and I don't need a man to tell me what to do.

Raj No, I didn't mean that.

Sunny I think you should go, Dark Ages man.

Raj But Sita!

Rani And now he's getting angry. Are you going to lash out at me next?

Raj Why are you saying that? Are you trying to provoke me?

Sunny Come on, mate, don't push your luck. Time to go.

Raj Sita?

[*Exit* **Raj**

Rani [*laughing*] Oh! Isn't he magnificent?! Impossible not to love a man like that.

Sunny [*laughing his head off*] Ah! ah! ah! ah!

Enter **Kamala-ji**

Kamala-ji I hear fun. What's all the laughter? Sunny?

Sunny We were just winding up Raj, that's all. [*To* **Kamala-ji**] I just threatened him a bit, you know, told him where to get off. It was a bit like Gangs of Wasseypur.

Kamala-ji Enough man-baiting now Rani, huh? Poor chap. He's come clean with you. So what are you putting him through now?

Sunny How far gone is lover boy, would you say, Rani?

Rani Oh, Sunny! Oh, Mummy! Let's just say I've got nothing to complain about.

Sunny Did you hear that? [*Imitating her*] Oh, Sunny, oh Mummy! Her voice went all breathy, like a late-night radio presenter. She must be in love, listeners. [**Rani** *doesn't deny it, just smiles at her mother.*]

Kamala-ji How wonderful! [**Rani** *smiles and nods*] So what's the plan? Get him to propose to you in your disguise? Without knowing who you are? Throw his whole life away for you, that sort of thing?

Rani Yes Ma, how did you guess?

Sunny [*laughing his head off*] Oh, neat, neat! You player! What are you? A player! Yesss! One mean mistress of pain!

Rani Alright, Sunny. Don't get carried away.

Sunny Ah! ah! It was fun when you were all miserable, but this is even better.

Kamala-ji Alright, then count me in. What do you need? Do you want me to be very disapproving and challenge him? Get insulted? Write to his dad?

Rani No, Ma, it won't be necessary. Oh Mummy, this was meant to be. It's so good it happened like this. Whenever he remembers how we met, he'll remember how much he wanted me today. And how much he was willing to give up to get me. It's going to make it a very special marriage. Unique. We won't be like other people, everything will always be perfect, because of today. Oh I'm so lucky, I'm so happy . . .

Sunny Aaaah! And they all lived happily ever after, and they never ever had a row or anything like that, because Rani tricked Raj into falling in love with her. Perfect. [*Sings*] Two for chai, and chai for two, you for me and me for you . . .

Kamala-ji Yes, the whole problem with fairy stories is what happens after the happy ending.

Rani Oh, don't be so cynical you two. Raj is mine. I can't wait to see him again.

Sunny Do you know, thinking of how he is suffering right now, I find it all rather moving.

Rani You're right, for once, Sunny. The more he suffers for it now, the more grateful he'll be for the rest of his life. He thinks he's going to upset his family, my family . . . And that's before the possible financial implications. Oh, he's got a big decision to make. A battle between his head and his heart, between common sense and his emotions.

Sunny And we know which of those we want to win, don't we.

Kamala-ji No self-esteem problems for my daughter, then, huh?

Sunny Strange how love can bring about such a huge disregard for the suffering of others, isn't it?

Enter **Sita**

Kamala-ji Ssshh, here comes Sita.

Sita Auntie-ji? You said earlier that I could do whatever I wanted with Raj Sharma. Well, I have. I've chopped him up, stirred him, heated him up and I think now, he's just about cooked. So, I've come to ask, does cousin Rani want him? Last chance.

Kamala-ji Rani?

Rani You're welcome Seets. I'm not interested in a recipe that I haven't personally prepared.

Sita So you agree, I can have him? And Auntie-ji, you agree too?

Kamala-ji If he loves you, why not? And good luck to him.

Sunny For my part, I agree to it too.

Rani Thank you Sunny. Shut up now.

Sita Oh yessss! Thank you, thank you, thank you! All of you. [*She hugs* **Kamala-ji**.]

Kamala-ji Just one thing. To avoid any recriminations later. Don't you think you should give him a little hint, a soupçon perhaps, of who you really are?

Sita But that would curdle the whole dish.

Kamala-ji So what? I'm sure he'll be able to take it.

[**Nitin** *starts to enter but stands to one side.*]

Sita Oh, here he comes! Do you mind leaving us alone for a minute? I've got to sprinkle him with garam masala.

Kamala-ji Of course, of course. Come along children.

Rani Good luck Sita.

Sunny Can I stay and watch and learn?

Rani No you bloody can't!

Kamala-ji Sunny! Chalo!

[*Exit* **Kamala-ji**, **Sunny** *and* **Rani**

Enter **Nitin**

Nitin Aaaah! Meri jaan! Meri choti Rani! There you are! I have been searching for you, my queen. Every moment away from you is torture! Torch-aah! I'll never leave your side for a single second again. I thought you were avoiding me.

Sita How do you know I wasn't?

Perhaps there is music heard distantly from another room in the house.

Nitin What? If I thought that was true I'd . . . I'd throw myself under a car. [*Singing the song 'Doob ke dariya mein' from the film 'Saajan Chale Sasural*'] Gaadi ke neeche aake, kar lungi khudkhushi. ['*By coming under a car, I'll commit suicide*']

Sita No, don't do that! Don't do that! If you did that, I'd jump into the sea.

Nitin Oh, how I love hearing you say that!

Sita [*She sings*] 'Doob ke dariya main, kar lungi khudkushi.' ['*By jumping into the sea I'll commit suicide.*']

Nitin Same! Same!

Sita I can't believe you know that film! Oh that's so beautiful.

Nitin Aaah! I wish I could eat up every one of those little, little words, as they come sploshing out of your mouth!

[*The music has faded away.*]

Sita Right. Now, you know you said you wanted to marry me but I said I'd have to ask my auntie? . . . I mean mother! I'd have to ask my mother, first? Well, I just spoke to her and she said OK!

Nitin Oh my love! That's, that's wonderful! [*A doubt occurs to him.*]

Sita Yes. I'm the luckiest girl in the world. You are so much more than I deserve. Much more than you know. So I want to tell you something . . .

Nitin No no, it is you, you who are worth so much more than me. Really. Listen . . .

Sita You give me more than I could ever have asked for.

Nitin Um, yeah, that's not, strictly speaking accurate. Believe me, I've done the maths.

Sita I see your love as a gift from heaven.

Nitin Yup, heaven can certainly afford it, I'm quite cheap.

Sita You're so classy, so dazzling, so successful!

Nitin Ah, but all that glitters is not gold. Don't forget that. It's a very useful cliché, that one.

Sita Don't be so modest.

Nitin Well, at least I had these few precious moments with you. That's what counts.

Sita What's the matter with you? Why have you gone all quiet?

Nitin I'm shy.

Sita Sorry?

Nitin I'm SHY! That's the funny thing about getting to know me, you see. You never know what you'll find at the bottom of the barrel.

Sita What are you trying to say, Raj, my lord?

Nitin I think we need to have a conversation.

Sita We're having a conversation.

Nitin Erm, erm, I need to be brought out of my shell, you see? To find the real me?

Sita My God! You don't want space already do you? That was quick!

Nitin [*aside*] Best approach this with a bit of lateral thinking. [*To* **Sita**] Have you ever heard of bouncing a cheque?

Sita What?

Nitin Counterfeit bank-note? Forged Picasso? Oh dear. This isn't easy. How big is your love for me?

Sita It's huge, it's huge.

Nitin So, do you think it could get by in a house with fewer rooms than it's used to?

Sita How many rooms?

Nitin Say, one, for example. Well, more like a studio flat with a pull down bed and a leaky cistern and something weird in the fridge that's been there for like, two years.

Sita What are you trying to tell me? Who are you? What is your name, Mister?

Nitin My name? [*Aside*] Should I tell her my real name which is Shankar? No, I know what it rhymes with, let's not go there.

Sita Well?

Nitin How do you like racing drivers?

Sita What do you mean racing drivers?

Nitin Well, more like, drivers in general really.

Sita What like truck drivers? [*Shakes his head*] Police drivers? [*Shakes his head again*] Bus drivers?

Nitin Getting warmer.

Sita Taxi drivers?

Nitin Not quite as good as that. I'm an unlicensed Uber driver.

Sita So you are not Raj Sharma?

Nitin He's my boss. Well, a regular customer. He doesn't know about the license thing, so . . .

Sita You toad! So you're not a banker.

Nitin No but my name does rhyme with banker. Among other things. Nitin Shankar. At your service, ma'am.

Sita You little snake!

Nitin Er, yeah. Can we flip the topic now?

Sita I can't believe I've spent all this time trying to impress this odious reptile. You shit!

Nitin Rani! Please let me say! I could make you just as happy as any hedge-fund guy, or property man, or doctor or lawyer, or any of the coveted professions. If you just put your feelings above your possessions. You have the greatest possession ever, mera dil, Rani, my heart. [**Sita** *suddenly bursts into laughter.*] What are you laughing at, skilful and gracious lady?

Sita I knew this would happen, I knew it! It always does to me. I've had hand-me-downs all my life. This is one hand-me-down I'm hanging on to. OK, I forgive you.

Nitin What just like that?

Sita No, more like this. [*She grabs him and pushes him into a massive sexy kiss with tongues and gropes his arse. Then, when she's done, she flings him away. He is breathless.*] So, tell me. How do you feel about beauticians?

Nitin Eh?

Sita Girls who work in beauty parlours. You know; pedicure, manicure, facials, threading, waxing, shellack.

Nitin Shellack?

Sita On the nails. Do you like 'em?

Nitin What? Urr . . . yeah. Like foxy nail varnish. With like, different colours. Yeah, I like it.

Sita Oh good. Because I'm Rani's poor little cousin Sita. I work in a beauty parlour six days a week except Wednesday afternoons. Go on, take your revenge. You can laugh at me now.

Nitin So, snake and shellack. That's us?

Sita Yup, that's it. A reptile and a hot towel. But let's get to the point. Do you love me?

Nitin Do I love you? Do I LOVE you? Of course I do. Your name may have changed, but you're still you. I love your eyes . . .

Sita Yup, they're still up here actually. That's better. Go on.

Nitin I love your teeth. I love your ears. I love your fingers. Let's not get in a state about what we haven't got, who we are not, and where we haven't been. Yet. Let's just shout to the world . . . [*He starts shouting 'I love you' but* **Sita** *stops him.*]

Sita Shh, sshh, quiet! Let's not! Let's not tell the others anything. It'll be our secret. Just for a little bit longer.

Nitin Oh yes! Great idea. Tss tss. Tee hee. [*They both start sniggering and giggling.*]

Sita And now, I must go to the lady's room and do lady's things, Mr Raj Sharma.

Nitin Oh Rani, my posh love! Don't be long, I cannot bear to be without you . . . tss tss. I'll just make some important long distance important business calls while you're gone.

[*Exit* **Sita**

Enter **Raj**, *at speed*

Nitin Oh hello, Sahib.

Raj Have you told her yet? Mrs Arora's daughter. Have you come clean?

Nitin Of course I have! I don't hang about. And you know what? She was totally cool about it. Yeah. Didn't bat an eyelid. In fact, when I told her I was driving you, d'you know what she said? She said; 'at least you get your petrol paid for.'

Raj Oh yeah?

Nitin Yeah, and then she said; 'I hope he tips well.' And I said, 'well actually, he doesn't bloody tip at all . . .'

Raj What rubbish are you spouting now?

Nitin So I think we're going to go ahead with the marriage.

Raj What? She agreed to marry you? Seriously?

Nitin What can I say? She's a classy lady.

Raj You didn't tell her, did you? Go on, admit it.

Nitin Mate! Bhai! Not so frequent with the patronizing remarks! Do you mind? I don't need you dissing me all the time, know what I mean? I may not be worth as much as you, but I'm worth twice as much as you.

Raj Sorry?

Nitin To her, I meant. I'm worth loads to her.

Raj You liar. I'm going to tell Mrs Arora.

Nitin [*imitating sing-song voice*] 'Na na ni na naa. I'm going to tell Mrs Arora.' You're going to tell my mother-in-law, huh? Lovely woman. So thoughtful. She's all for it, as it happens.

Raj You talk absolute drivel, you know that? Now, do you know where Sita is?

Nitin Sita? The poor little cousin girl? She may have walked right by me, but you know what, I just can't remember. Not interested. You're welcome to her.

Raj Oh, go and put your head in a bucket of cold water. You're over-heating.

Nitin It's sad really, isn't it, how people can get so used to ordering other people about that they completely lose touch. Spoilt, I suppose. Ah well, I'm off . . . . Oh I was just thinking – you're good with figures – when I'm married, I'll be needing someone to do my book-keeping, would you like the position?

Raj Piss off!

Nitin Just going.

Enter **Rani**

Nitin Sita, my dear soon-to-be cousin! My driver, South, here was just asking after you. Pining even. Ta-ta.

[*Exit* **Nitin**

Rani South! Where've you been? I've been looking for you to tell you what Mrs Arora-ji said.

Raj Well, as you can see, I haven't gone yet. Sorry.

Rani Ooh, so cold. Sulking now.

Raj So, what's the problem now?

Rani I told Mrs Arora-ji everything about your idiot driver and her daughter and I suggested that at the very least she should postpone the wedding. But you know what? She just poo-pooed me, waved me away and said she was booking a marquee for as soon as possible.

Raj Oh, right.

Rani So now would be a good time to tell her.

Raj Tell her what?

Rani Of your intentions.

The Game of Love and Chai   Act Two   61

Raj   What intentions would those be, Sita? You made it quite clear where I stand with you. You and Sunny did that, in no uncertain terms. I'll just leave a note for Mrs Arora explaining that it's all my fault, it was a stupid prank that went wrong, and then I'll slip away quietly.

Rani   Oh no. That's not right. [*Aside*] That's not what I want to happen.

Raj   Don't you think it'd be for the best?

Rani   No, not really.

Raj   I'm sorry, but I can't think of anything better under the circumstances. I can't bear to hang around and witness the outcome of my stupid games. I'm sorry.

Rani   What do you mean?

Raj   You know what I mean, Sita.

Rani   What? That you don't like Mrs Arora-ji's daughter, is that it?

Raj   Oh come on, Sita, you know it's not that.

Rani   Well, what then?

Raj   Goodbye Sita, I'm sorry.

Rani   What! Seriously, you're leaving?

Raj   You seem worried that I might change my mind.

Rani   How would you know what I'm worried about?

Raj   You want to get rid of me that much? Bye Sita.

Rani [*aside*] Oh god! If he actually leaves now, that's it, I'm finished with him! He's got to want me more than that. [*She looks at him going*] Oh! He's stopping!... He's thinking . . . he's looking to see if I turn my head round, but I'm . . . not . . . going to! It'd actually be rather selfish of him to go now, after everything we've been through! . . . Ah! Well that's it then. It's all over, he's gone; I don't have as much power over him as I thought. It's all Sunny's fault! Bloody insensitive clumsy,

Rani (*cont.*)   brother of mine! . . . Oh but here he is again! He's coming back! I take away what I said; I still love him . . . Let's pretend to be leaving so he can stop me . . .

Raj   Please! There was one last thing I wanted to say.

Rani   What? To me? . . . or . . .? [*She looks over her shoulder as if there might be someone else there.*]

Raj   I don't feel I can leave until I've made you understand that it really is the right thing to do.

Rani   That's pathetic. So, I'm just the poor little cousin, the fly on the wall. The one who gets buffeted around and crushed in all the important people's grand affairs. Don't mind me.

Raj   But Sita! Can't you see that I'm just trying to be a man and face up to the inevitable?

Rani   I don't think I'm in a position to answer that question. You have no idea what it's like having no status, firstly as a woman, but secondly in this family. I have no family of my own. Auntie-ji took me in and I'm very grateful. She's been so generous to me.

Raj   And so that's why you want to get together with Sunny?

Rani   Maybe.

Raj   I saw it myself, earlier on. You just wanted me out of the way so that you could be with him.

Rani   What exactly did you see earlier on? Hmm? How would you know what I feel? You have no idea what is at stake for me here.

Raj   Well then, Sita, please, I beg you, tell me. Tell me what you really feel.

Rani   What's the point, when you're about to leave?

Raj   Alright I'll stay. I'll stay.

Rani Leave me alone. If you really loved me, you wouldn't question me like this. You wouldn't need all this reassurance. You're just scared of rejection. What do you really care about my feelings?

Raj Your feelings are all I care about Sita, believe me. I'm crazy about you.

Rani Yes, you've said that so often. But what do you expect me to do about it? OK, I'm going to be frank with you. You say you love me, but for you, there are so many ways of wriggling out of it! You, a man with all the status, all the money and all the choices. You can fall in love with some poor girl one minute, and then out of it again the next. Life makes it easier for someone like you . . .

Raj That's not fair.

Rani Shut up a minute, I'm talking. Think of who I am, and who you are. The distance there is between us. The thousands of women you'll meet who can give you so much more than I can. The amusements and distractions that are available to a man like you. That could wear down your love. The way you'll be able to laugh it all off when you get bored with me. Think of that.

Raj I'd never get bored.

Rani But what of me? If I commit myself, what will be the consequences of that? You may have all the money and all the power, but I have so much more to lose than you. I have nothing but my heart. Who would compensate me for your loss? You could just pick me up, use me and discard me as you pleased and where would that leave me? If you knew what I was really feeling, you'd go mad. So I'm keeping my feelings to myself, as I hope you will be kind enough to do too.

Raj Oh Sita! What is all this? Your words burn me up. All the money in the world, my career, my family, everything comes second to you. I don't care about any of all that. I just want you. Here, my hand. It has my heart in it.

Rani [*pleased*] Oh gosh. I don't know how much longer I can keep this up.

Raj You love me then?

Rani I didn't say that. But if you ask me one more time, there's no telling what might happen to you.

Raj I'm not afraid of your threats. But what about Sunny?

Rani But what about Sunny? Aren't you a bit afraid of him?

Raj Sunny? You're joking. I know you love me. I just know it. All the rest of this is . . . is just bullshit. I love you Sita.

Rani Oh! I see. And what are you going to do about it? If anything.

Raj Sita. Will you marry me?

Rani [*delighted like a little girl*] Aaaahhhgggg!!! What about your family?! What about Mu [*Correcting herself*] . . . I mean Auntie-ji? You want to marry me despite who you are, despite your father's anger, despite all your loads of money?

Raj Yeah, yeah, yeah. 'course I do. What does your heart say?

Rani It's thinking about it.

Raj Don't think, feel.

Rani You will never change your mind?

Raj No.

Rani [*sighs*] Oh!

> *Enter* **Kamala-ji, Sunny, Sita** *and* **Nitin**
> *with flowers*

Rani Ah! You told me to check him out, Ma. So I did . . . And he's alright. More than alright.

Raj What? You're her mother, ji?

Kamala-ji Erm, yes. Sorry about that, old chap. Namaskar.

Rani Yes, Raj. We both had the same idea for getting to know each other. And it worked.

Kamala-ji Your dad sent me this letter, huh? But I never showed it to Rani, she found you out all by herself.

Raj Oh my God. That is amazing. You beat me at my own game! I'm just relieved that I passed the test!

Sunny Yeah, like, I'm sorry bhai, if I gave you any grief.

Raj No need to be sorry, I'm grateful. Bhai. I am so happy.

Nitin [*to* **Sita**] And you my treasure, you are the luckiest one of all! You get ME!

Sita Yeah I got you alright. And don't you forget it.

[*Music strikes up*]

Rani What has happened to me? What is this restless intoxication? Ask me, just ask me! Ah! *Puchho zara Puchho!* It's punishment for falling in love! Ask me, just ask me! I will always give you the same answer. This love is its own reward.

They all dance and mime the finale to 'Puchho Zara Puchho' [from the film 'Raja Hindustani']

> *puchho zara puchho mujhe kya huva hai*
> *kaisi bekaaraari hai ye kaisa nasha hai*
> *tumase dil lagaane ki saja hai*
> *rajaaji tumase dil lagaane ki saja hai*
>
> *puchho zara puchho mujhe kya huva hai*
> *kaisi bekaaraari hai ye kaisa nasha hai*
> *tumase dil lagaane ki saja hai*
> *rootha hai kyon raja kyon mujhase khafa hai*

END

I, An Actor

by Nicholas Craig with
Christopher Douglas & Nigel Planer

Foreword by Steve Coogan

'a brilliantly funny and astute look at the world of theatre'
Harriett Gilbert, BBC Radio 4's A Good Read, October 2017

From the foreword:

"It is 2011. I am in a pretty comfortable place, a small manor house nestled in those bosomy mounds more commonly known as the South Downs, I have the requisite pied à terre and a retreat in 'The Lakes' where I like to wander lonely as the proverbial cloud. I have ticked every box in the world of comedy, more awards than I know what to do with (I keep them in my awards shed/smoking room) and five BAFTAs that smile at me yet, like a mocking Greek chorus, seem to say, 'Well, Steve, happy now?'. I am not. Yes I've made people the length and breadth of Britain laugh, and some Americans, but there is a hole, an ache, a hunger, a thirst and I mean to sate it, or die trying. I WANT TO MAKE PEOPLE CRY. I discuss this with my gardener, who reads the *TLS* and *The Guardian*. He smiles as he leans on a hoe or something whilst rolling a cigarette. 'What you're saying . . . is . . . you want to ACT'. 'Yes, yes, that's it!' I yelp. 'Then . . . ,' he begins, sauntering off toward my compost bins made from reclaimed wood, 'you'd better call Nicholas Craig.' He says it with a kind of wise divine certainty that bestowed on me a kind of clarity that was almost damascene. 'Of course, I will call Nick.' All is well, and all will be well."

Another great actor explores himself and his profession in this terrifically scathing parody of the theatrical memoir. Hilarious, vindictive and very accurate. Startlingly truthful, unflinchingly illustrated, *I, An Actor* is a piton up the slope of creativity for theatre fans and aspiring actors alike, revealing everything that most theatrical autobiographies cravenly avoid.

ISBN: 978 0413 777263   November 2016   £12.99